SOUTHERN COLORADO

4-W

THE

Descriptions and maps of
25 spectacular 4-wheel drive routes
in the mountains around
Telluride, Ouray, Silverton,
& Lake City, Colorado.

Wayne W. Griffin

WHO PRESS
BASALT, COLORADO

PUBLISHED BY

WHO Press
0311 West Sopris Creek Road
Basalt, Colorado 81621

Library of Congress Catalog Card Number: 98-60848
ISBN 1-882426-07-X
Printed in the United States of America

Photos by Wayne Griffin & Billie Shafer
Cover photo by Wayne Griffin

Cover design by Curt Carpenter
Maps by Warren H. Ohlrich
Edited by Warren H. Ohlrich

Table of Contents

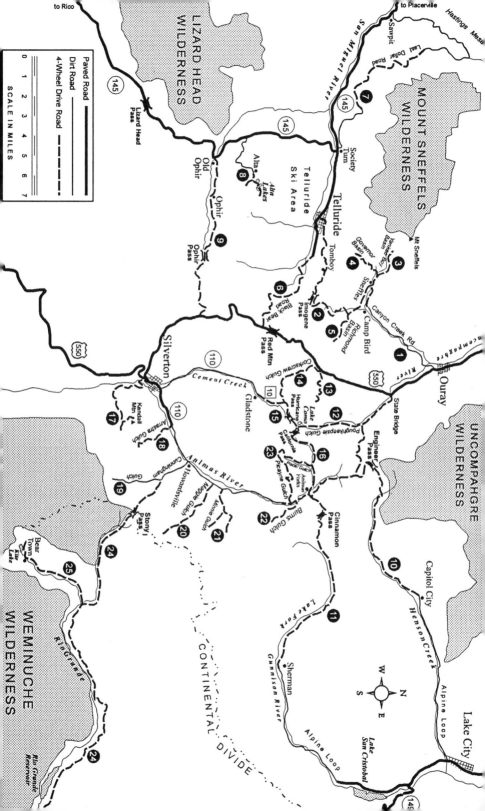

Introduction

The mountains of southwestern Colorado, known as the San Juans, offer some of the most spectacular scenery in Colorado, if not in the entire United States. To the south of Montrose, the once popular supply and railroad town, the area known as the San Juans starts to unfold. The open space of the flat valley merges into hills covered with pinion and scrub oak, and by Ridgway the mountains of the San Juans loom ahead. The area to the right is known as the Sneffels Range, highlighted by Mount Sneffels (14,150 feet), Potosi Peak, Teakettle Mountain, Whitehouse Mountain, Cirque and Stony mountains, to name a few. On the left lie Courthouse Mountain, Sneva, Dunsinane, and Blackwall mountains, along with Wetterhorn, Matterhorn, Coxcomb, and Uncompahgre peaks.

These mountains of the San Juans were created from volcanic activity approximately 35 million years ago and are believed to be some of the youngest in the Rocky Mountain chain. Due to their volcanic origin they also harbor some of the richest mineral deposits discovered by man, including gold, silver, copper, zinc, and other precious metals. It is because of these riches that prospectors and the adventuresome were drawn to the area starting in the early 1860s. Mines sprung up on almost every mountainside with paths, which eventually became roads, for transporting supplies to the mine areas and the ore back to the mills and towns. These towns remain a part of the San Juans today; some are small communities, others exist only as historic ghost towns, and a few have become major recreational centers.

The mining roads have become the 4-wheelers playground, offering not only a challenge, but routes to some of the most spectacular scenic beauty imaginable. They access high mountain passes, spectacular mountain valleys, hidden ghost towns, numerous old and working mines, good fishing, camping, and scenic vistas not readily available to the average motorist. To participate in 4-wheel driving on these roads you do need a certain amount of skill, sensibility, and some good guidance. The purpose of this book is to describe the most popular routes for 4-wheeling in the San Juans, and to provide background information on 4-wheeling as an aid for route selection, route-finding, and safety.

Looking at the Sneffels Range from the top of Richmond Basin.

The roads described in this guide cover a wide range of difficulty. Several of the routes can be managed by a 2-wheel drive vehicle with careful driving, but 4-wheel vehicles are recommended due to their higher clearance and 4-wheel traction, which make the journey easier with less worry about undercarriage damage. Although this guidebook describes the difficulty of each trail, difficulty ratings can never be standardized. They depend as much on the driver's ability, the type of vehicle being driven, and the equipment on the vehicle, as on the route itself. Weather conditions, especially rain or high mountain snows, can drastically affect the difficulty of the route; roads can become slick and impassable after a storm. Any description of the difficulty of a route should be accepted as only a starting point. It is always best to talk to other drivers or authorities who have been on the route, including the Forest Service and the County Sheriff's Office.

The heading information for each route lists the text map, the National Forest maps, USGS 7.5-minute quadrangle contour maps, and the Trail Illustrated maps which apply to that particular route. At a minimum, you should always carry the appropriate National Forest map and the Trails Illustrated map (#141) for Silverton, Ouray, Telluride, and Lake City.

The San Juans span four National Forests: the San Juan National Forest, the Uncompahgre National Forest, the Gunnison National Forest, and the Rio Grande National Forest. The USGS maps give greater detail and contour elevations, and are especially helpful for finding out-of-the-way places and historic sites. The Trails Illustrated map has the most current and detailed information, and is probably the most important map to have along. Getting sidetracked and off the beaten path can happen on any route. It is beyond the scope of this book to cover every possible turnoff and side road or trail, so take along as many maps as possible.

Certain inherent dangers exist in the backcountry. Road conditions constantly change and many of the routes can be very difficult and dangerous, especially for inexperienced 4-wheelers. Before setting out on any trip, you should always check with the U.S. Forest Service or the County Sheriff's Office for route conditions, accessibility of routes, and weather. It is also a good idea to inform a friend or associate, who is not venturing with you, of the routes you intend to take and approximate time of return, just in case something unexpected occurs on your trip in the backcountry.

Always carry plenty of food, emergency rations, and water. Other essential items, especially for longer and more difficult routes, include: a hydraulic or handyman jack, first aid kit, fire extinguisher, tow strap, shovel, flashlights and extra batteries, fire starters and matches, dry clothes, blankets or sleeping bags, and work gloves. Even though your plans may only be for a day trip, you never know when breakdowns, getting lost, or accidents may extend your stay in the sometimes very unforgiving high country.

The U.S. Forest Service puts out a small book entitled *4-Wheeling* which contains lots of good information on safety, winching, backroad savvy, and other critical areas of 4-wheel driving. The book is free and should be available in any Forest Service office.

Backcountry 4-Wheeling Ethics

It is a privilege that we are given the opportunity to travel the backcountry in order to enjoy its breathtaking mountain views, scenic valleys, secluded lakes, wildlife, and historic value. Therefore, certain ethical rules need to be followed so we can preserve the backcountry experience for others and future generations.

1. Follow the Tread Lightly Program, which means Travel only on designated routes; Respect the rights of others; Educate yourself; Avoid driving across open meadows and streams, pursuing wildlife in your vehicle, etc.; Drive and travel responsibly. The vegetation and soil in the backcountry is easily destroyed, so limiting travel to established roads will allow others to enjoy the unmarred land as you see it. Simply put, stay on traveled paths, don't cut switchbacks, don't drive through open meadows, and definitely don't drive across alpine tundra.

2. Preserve America's heritage by not disturbing old mining camps, cabins, ghost towns, or other historical features.

3. Leave rocks, flowers, wood, antlers, and artifacts in their natural state for others to enjoy.

4. Respect the rights and property of others. Miners, recreationists, ranchers, fishermen, hunters, and others rely on the backcountry for enjoyment and livelihood.

5. Get permission before you cross private land. Leave gates as you find them.

6. Take out what you brought in, and if you find litter take it with you. Encourage others to keep a clean camp by doing more than your share to rid the backcountry of litter.

7. Safety and courtesy are contagious. Spread them around.

8. Leave your dogs at home or keep them under control when they are not in the vehicle. Your dog doesn't know not to chase cows, sheep, or wild animals, which could be harmful for these creatures. You also want to get along with fellow backcountry enthusiasts and not annoy them, so use a leash if necessary.

9. Listen to the silence. Avoid noise pollution.

10. Camp in an existing site whenever possible, away from stream banks and lakeshores. Cook your meals on a cookstove, unless you have an established fire ring and the proper utensils for cooking over an open fire. If you use an open fire make sure you have plenty of water to douse all of the burning embers. It only takes one spark to destroy a forest.

11. Carry a light digging tool for proper disposal of human waste.

12. When bathing or washing utensils, use biodegradable soaps and dispose of waste water properly, away from lakes and streams.

13. Proper use of a winch can help reduce adverse environmental impact on vegetation and the land. Generally, a winch should be used for emergency situations and to overcome temporary natural barriers such as fallen trees, landslides, and damaged stream crossings. When using a winch in connection with a tree, make sure the tree is alive, big enough to withstand the strain, and always use a tree strap.

14. If you encounter other recreationists who may not appreciate your 4-wheel drive vehicle sharing their backcountry experience, keep in mind that backcountry travel has increased substantially over the past few years as more people want to get away from the masses. Everyone has the same right to use the backcountry roads. Be as polite as possible and always use common sense.

With the increased use of the backcountry we all must assume the responsibility for the environment and our impact on it. Remembering these simple, easy-to-follow guidelines will help everyone enjoy the backcountry environment and have a pleasant experience.

Backcountry traffic on Engineer Pass Road.

Rules of the Road

1. Rules of the highway also apply to most out-of-the-way, primitive backcountry roads, so use the same precautions and rules that you do in everyday driving.

2. Since there are very few speed signs on backcountry roads it is your responsibility to keep your speed under control. Hazards can exist at every turn and the scenery is best enjoyed at a slower pace.

3. There are no stop signs or street lights at backcountry intersections, so always be ready to yield.

4. When being overtaken by another vehicle whose pace is quicker than yours, pull over at a safe point and let it by.

5. Vehicles coming uphill have the right-of-way; it's easier and safer to back up than to back down. However, the vehicle which is closer to a wide place in the road, no matter which direction it is traveling, should move over in order to let the other vehicle pass.

6. When you leave your vehicle, park it in a safe place completely off the traveled part of the roadway. Make sure your parking brake is set and will hold the vehicle in place. For added security wedge rocks under the wheels to prevent a runaway vehicle. Turn your wheels in a direction so the vehicle will run into a bank should it break loose and start rolling.

Tips on 4-Wheel Driving

1. Most 4-wheel drive vehicles have two different 4-wheel drive gear ratios. Once you leave the pavement you will want to make sure your transfer case is either in 4-wheel high or 4-wheel low, depending upon the difficulty of the route. On gravel roads of easy to moderate difficulty, 4-wheel high gives you additional traction. However, on more difficult terrain the gear ratio may be too high and 4-wheel low should be used.

2. Backcountry roads which were originally wagon routes can be extremely rough with boulder fields and sharp protruding rocks. Use caution and maneuver your vehicle through these areas, like skiing a slalom course. When the road is extremely narrow and you cannot maneuver around a rock sufficiently, it is best to drive directly over the rock, since there is more rubber and support at the tread of the tire than at the sidewall. If you try to avoid sharp rocks by maneuvering in limited space, the results could be a punctured sidewall and a tire change.

3. If you have the misfortune of experiencing a tire problem, drive slowly to a point where you can safely pull to the side of the road so other vehicles may pass. Tires sometimes need to be changed in precarious positions, so always block the good tires with rocks to prevent the vehicle from rolling when jacked up, and put on the emergency brake. A word of caution—make sure you have a good spare tire, a jack, and a tire tool before starting out. Should you have a mishap, this could prevent a long walk back to town and embarrassment.

4. Always drive within the limitations of the road. Don't take unnecessary risks for you and your passengers.

5. When descending steep terrain, make sure your vehicle is in low range and select a gear which allows you to keep your foot off the brake as much as possible. This will save the brakes.

6. When descending a steep backcountry road after a rain or snow storm, make sure the vehicle is in low range and first gear before attempting the descent. Keep your foot off the brake. If the soil is slippery, or mud or snow covers the road, braking is one of the worst things you could do—it turns your 4-wheel drive vehicle into a sled over which you have no control.

12

7. When attempting a water crossing, know the depth of the puddle or stream. This can be checked by any long object—a shovel, tree branch, etc. Stalling in deep water may risk engine damage due to water backup through the exhaust system.

8. During a lightning storm, your safest place is in your rubber-tired enclosed cab vehicle. Avoid open ridges, lone trees, and rock outcrops. Seek shelter in dense stands of trees, deep valleys, or at the foot of a cliff.

Rollover on the switchbacks of Black Bear Road.

Tips on Survival

1. Letting a responsible person know where you are going and approximately what time to expect your return is probably the most important aspect of 4-wheeling, and in some cases may even save your life.

2. Know where you are at all times through a map and reference points or the use of GPS equipment and a GPS map. Remember the route you followed in, just in case you have to follow it out.

3. Always make sure to carry plenty of provisional supplies, the most crucial being water. You can survive a number of days without food; however, in extreme conditions and high altitude you could possibly die within three days without water. Should it become necessary to drink water from a stream or lake you may want to have along some iodine, since it is the easiest method for sterilizing the water. It might not look, smell or taste very good, but it will kill the bacteria which could make you very sick.

4. If you are stranded without food and not familiar with vegetation which is safe to eat, you will be better off eating nothing to avoid getting extremely ill, or worse.

5. Always carry the essentials like waterproof matches (or matches in a waterproof container), a map and compass, a pocket knife (preferably a Swiss army knife), a first aid kit, nylon cord, extra food, a flashlight (with spare batteries), at least a one-quart water bottle (full), and a garbage bag, poncho, or waterproof insulated clothing to keep you dry or act as an insulating layer between you and the elements.

6. The most important thing to take along is your common sense. In difficult situations using your head is what counts the most. Use the four S's: Stop, Sit, and Size up the Situation.

Important Addresses and Telephone Numbers

San Juan National Forest

Columbine Ranger District
701 Camino del Rio
Durango, Co. 81301
(970) 247-4874

Gunnison National Forest

Taylor-Cebolla Ranger District
216 N. Colorado
Gunnison, Co. 81230
(970) 641-0471

Ouray Ranger District
2505 South Townsend
Montrose, Co. 81401
(970) 240-5300

Taylor-Cebolla Ranger District
Lake City Office
P.O. Box 430
Lake City, Co. 81235
(970) 944-2527

Rio Grande National Forest

Divide Ranger District
3rd and Creede Avenue
P.O. Box 270
Creede, Co. 81130
(719) 658-2556

San Juan National Forest

Mancos-Dolores Ranger District
P.O. Box 210
Dolores, Co. 81323
(970) 882-7296

Ouray Ranger District (see above)

Uncompahgre National Forest

Norwood Ranger District
P.O. Box 388
Norwood, Co. 81423
(970) 327-4261

County Sheriffs' Offices

Gunnison County Sheriff's Office
(970) 641-1113

Hinsdale County Sheriff's Office
(970) 944-2291

San Juan County Sheriff's Office
(970) 387-5531

Ouray County Sheriff's Office
(970) 325-7272

San Miguel County Sheriff's Office
(970) 728-3081

Mineral County Sheriff's Office
(719) 658-2600

Trail Ratings

#1 Gravel road maintained by county jurisdiction. Passable by 2-wheel drive vehicles.

#2 Gravel road periodically maintained with small ruts and some obstacles.

#3 Dirt road with some occasional maintenance; weather conditions can create ruts and otherwise influence the condition of the road. Small rocks or holes exist which require some maneuvering.

#4 Road may be partially maintained; however, it has several areas of difficulty which may include stream crossings and small rock fields. Weather conditions may cause mud holes and extreme ruts which create the need for high clearance and 4-wheel drive capability.

#5 Road is well traveled, but rock fields are more prevalent. Weather conditions can create major obstacles, and some driving technique is required.

#6 Road is not maintained. Rocks and other obstacles create several difficult areas requiring maneuverability to successfully reach your destination. Obstacles should be checked for depth. Wide vehicles may be restricted due to narrow passage.

#7 Road becomes rough with many obstacles like deep stream crossings and small boulder fields to cross. These roads are narrow and require a good knowledge of all the backcountry techniques described earlier in this guide.

#8 Road is fairly rough throughout with some space between rock fields, requiring substantial maneuverability. These roads are very narrow with stream crossings, steep drop-offs, and steep ascents or descents. Proper equipment is essential.

#9 Road is very rough and challenging from the onset. Rock fields are close together with many obstacles, requiring substantial maneuverability. The rock fields contain large, sharp boulders, but are separated by patches of smoother road. These roads have surface of loose shell rock in some areas combined with steep drop-offs.

#10 Extremely difficult. Road is a continuous challenge with boulder fields or loose shell rock over the majority of the route. The route consists of extremely narrow paths with steep drop-offs (500 to 1500 feet). Stream crossings are more difficult, and obstacles are prevalent around every corner. It is always advisable to have more than one vehicle when encountering this type of terrain. Road conditions are easily made more difficult by weather.

"Pucker Point" on Black Bear Road.

A Brief History of the San Juan Area

Today we think of the San Juans as skiing in Telluride, soaking the cold from our bones in the hot springs of Ouray, snowmobiling in Lake City, or the pure peaceful isolation of Silverton in the winter, and, of course, 4-wheeling the entire area in the summer. However, from the early 1860s through the mid 1870s thoughts were of prospecting and the fear of hostile Indians. The San Juans were, after all, Ute Indian Territory and most bands fought the white settlers who were heading west. Therefore, when Captain Charles Baker put together an expedition from Oro City and headed out in July of 1860 with six men for Fort Garland and west into the San Juans, he and his men were taking great risks. In search of new areas abundant in silver and gold, like the Cripple Creek or Leadville areas they had left, they crossed the eastern San Juans and set up camp in an alpine valley at 9,200 feet, building crude huts from logs and brush. Through the winter they lived in fear of hostile Indians, but when spring came they headed up the Animas Canyon panning for gold. They finally found some gold at a location close to what soon became the city of Eureka. The word traveled fast, the story became exaggerated, and it wasn't long before the area where the first crude structures were built became Baker City. Charles Baker didn't fare as well once the miners learned of the exaggerated claims he had made. The miners rebelled and Baker only saved himself from being lynched by fortunately panning and finding gold on the spot where they came to get him. Escaping back to his native Virginia, Baker returned in 1868 only to be killed by hostile Indians.

Development was slow and it wasn't until the Brunot Treaty of 1874, which forced the Utes to give up the land, that the area was opened for prospecting without fear. The stampede was on as more and more people headed west to seek their fortunes in mineral rich territories like the San Juans. Mining camps seemed to spring up in every gulch or valley, creating the need for supplies and the transport of ore back to the mills for processing. Towns started springing up and the mule trails turned into wagon roads, making it easier to transport larger amounts of supplies and ore. Transportation was still a major problem since these roads were extremely rough, taking an extreme toll on the wagons. Otto Mears came to the area in the early 1880s with the intention of opening a transportation network to help solve some of the transportation problems. Mears is most famous for his construction of the Durango to Silverton narrow gauge railroad; however, in the 1880s he was known as a master road builder and he was responsible for the opening up of the most popular transportation corridors of the San Juans. We can thank these early prospectors and men like Otto Mears for giving 4-wheelers this playground in the San Juans.

The area is referred to as the San Juans, even though the San Juan Range, San Juan National Forest, and San Juan County make up only a small part of this magnificent playground. When we speak of the San Juans we are talking of an area that stretches from Ouray, Colorado west to Telluride, east to Lake City, south to Silverton with an extension further southeast to Creede. These towns originated from the same roots, each different from the other, but the same in purpose.

The Camp Bird Mill.

Ouray

Ouray, Colorado, is located on the north end of the San Juans at the foot of Mount Abrams, in a natural basin along the Uncompahgre River. Founded by A. W. Begole and Jack Eckles in July, 1875, Ouray was originally named Uncompahgre City. However, the name was never accepted by the political officials working to change Colorado from a territory to a state, so it was renamed Ouray after the highly respected Ute Indian chief who helped bring peace to the area.

It didn't take long before mining claims were being filed within the present townsite, and miners like A.J. Staley and Logan Whitlock were literally stumbling into rich mining areas. Staley and Whitlock discovered the Trout and Fisherman lodes while on a fishing trip looking for a good hole. The first building in town was the Star Saloon where it is said whisky glasses were being used so fast there was no time to wash them. Prospectors were coming by the hundreds over Engineer, Imogene, and other passes, and from Montrose to the north via the Uncompahgre Valley.

Ouray was incorporated on October 2, 1876, and by winter it had more than 400 inhabitants. The town had grown to include a schoolhouse, four stores, two hotels, two blacksmith shops, a saw mill, a post office, thirty saloons, and numerous gambling houses. Prospectors had ventured into the vicinity of Mount Sneffels, where Andy Richardson found the extremely rich Camp Bird gold vein at the base of the Imogene Basin. They also fanned out into Yankee Boy Basin, Governor Basin, and Richmond Basin, creating mining activity everywhere. Most of the active mining in the area has long since passed, but Ouray, surrounded by 14,000-foot peaks, has become a fabulous getaway for tourists, and has been dubbed "The Switzerland of the Rockies".

Lake City

Lake City, Colorado, is located on the eastern edge of the San Juan area at the confluence of Henson Creek and the Lake Fork of the Gunnison River. Founded in 1874 by Enos Hotchkiss who discovered the "Golden Fleece" mine, the small encampment soon grew into a major connection for supplies, mail, and stagecoach service from the San Luis Valley to the mines around Ouray, Silverton, and Telluride. The name Lake City came from the largest natural body of water in the state of Colorado, Lake San Cristobal, located a few miles south of town. Like the other mining towns Lake City had its characters, but none were more famous than Alferd Packer who was found guilty of killing and cannibalizing five of his fellow companions during the winter of 1874. Today Lake City is a quiet little town with Victorian homes and log cabins lining the streets. It is a haven for snowmobiling in the winter, and fishing, camping, and 4-wheeling in the summer.

Telluride

Telluride, Colorado, is located on the western side of the San Juan area at the foot of a box canyon at the head of the San Miguel River Valley. The area saw its first settlers around 1875, and by 1876 the settlement named Columbia had 100 residents. By 1885 it was reported that Columbia had numerous stores of all types, a bank, two stamp mills, a weekly newspaper, and a booming population of approximately 1,400. In 1887 the town's name was changed to Telluride, possibly for the mineral Tellurium, but definitely because the U.S. Postal Department voiced an objection to having a second town named Columbia, since the name was already being used in California. The town grew and became a major supply source and ore processing center for the mines which had sprung up in the neighboring hillsides. When the Rio Grande Southern Railroad rolled into town in November, 1890, approximately 5,000 residents were calling Telluride their home. Following the Silver Crash of 1893 the population dropped; however, with the discovery of gold the population held firm at 3,000 through the gold boom days. The little town of Telluride grew into a Wild West mining town sporting 26 brothels or "parlor houses," at least 26 saloons, and 175 women employed in the red light district. Its history tells of Butch Cassidy's gang once holding up the San Miguel Valley Bank; a member of the Jesse James gang, Jim Clark, once served as deputy marshal while repeatedly breaking the law in other areas; and the remains of many outlaws can be found in the Lone Tree Cemetery. The town saw labor troubles with the unions, well-lighted streets using some of the first alternating current in the United States coming from the nearby Ames generating plant designed by George Westinghouse, and a Bank of Telluride executive who swindled the banks in New York out of $500,000.00 so that his clients didn't lose their hard earned money. Today Telluride has found riches in white gold, profiting from a bustling ski industry in the winter. The summers are marked by festivals and solitude.

Bridal Veil Falls above Telluride.

Silverton

Silverton, Colorado, is located on the southern end of the San Juans, along the Animas River in a large open area at 9,200 feet at the base of Kendall Mountain. Originally named Bakers Park after Captain Charles Baker who lead the first exploration party into the San Juans, Silverton was the first settlement in the area. The early settlers built crude huts for shelter and lived in fear of the Ute Indians. In 1874 the Brunot Treaty was signed and the Ute Indians were moved north to a reservation near Meeker, Colorado, and the area was opened to prospectors and settlers. In June of 1874 a town company was organized and Silverton began to take shape. By the mid 1880s several buildings lined main street, including the Grand Imperial Hotel, the San Juan County Court House, and the Congregational Church. These buildings have all been well maintained or restored, and stand as a symbol of the early days. Miners came in droves from the San Luis Valley and established mines and claims in every gulch and atop almost every hillside. With the success in this mineral rich area came the stamp mills, supply stores, and several railroads, including the Denver and Rio

Silverton with the Silverton-Durango train in the foreground.

Grande which still operates a daily schedule during the summer months from Durango to Silverton. During the winter months Silverton is routinely cut off from the outside world due to heavy snow and snowslides, but during the summer it offers more territory for 4-wheeling than any other area of the San Juans.

Imogene Basin and the Sneffels Mining District

Imogene Basin and the Sneffels Mining District was one of the most successful and productive mining areas in the San Juan Mountains. This area was first prospected by Andy Richardson and William Quinn around 1875. The basin at the head of the valley was named after Richardson's wife Imogene. Mines like the Ruby Trust and the Virginius employed 600 men and produced $1,000,000,000.00 worth of gold and silver by today's standards. Ore from these mines was first taken by mule and then by wagon over a saddle (now known as Imogene Pass) between Telluride Peak and Chicago Peak, then down the Savage Basin into Telluride. Imogene Pass is now the second highest vehicular pass in North America at 13,114 feet, second only to Mosquito Pass (13,186 feet) in Central Colorado (see *Central Colorado 4-Wheeling*).

Life in the valley was tough with severe winters and extremely hazardous snowslides. It is reported in one incident in the early 1900s that a snowslide claimed seven miners and twenty-seven horses and mules; other slides buried miners in their cabins and claimed the lives of their rescuers. After the Sherman Act of 1893 which demonetized silver, many of the mining camps in the Colorado Rockies started withering away. The Sneffels Mining District had a different fate. In the summer of 1895 Andy Richardson, now working as a scout for Tom Walsh of the Silverton area, set out with the belief that there was gold in the Sneffels area. After several days of prospecting Richardson came across a vein which appeared to be rich with the qualities associated with gold. Prospecting through the morning Richardson returned to his pack mule to retrieve his lunch, only to find it had been eaten by the birds we know as camp robbers (Canadian Jays), which lead Richardson and Walsh to name this strike the Camp Bird. The Camp Bird soon became one of the highest producers in the entire San Juan area.

One of the signs of the rich history of the San Juans.

The top of Imogene Pass yields a bird's-eye view of the entire San Juan area with the Sneffels Range to the north, and in the distance to the northwest the La Sal Mountains in Utah. On the Savage Basin side of the pass, at approximately 3,000 feet above Telluride, is the remains of the Tomboy Camp. Discovered in 1880, the Tomboy vein became a major gold producer in the basin. By 1894 the encampment at 11,500 feet was blossoming, and eventually reached the size of a small community with more than 250 miners' cabins and tents, a large 60-stamp mill, livery stables, a boarding house for 250 men, and even a bowling alley. Further on down the road, which once saw daily stagecoach traffic transporting passengers and mail between Telluride and Tomboy, the San Miguel River Valley opens up to spectacular views of Bridal Veil Falls to the south, the switchbacks of Black Bear Pass, and Ingram Falls on the eastern headwall. The town of Telluride is just below.

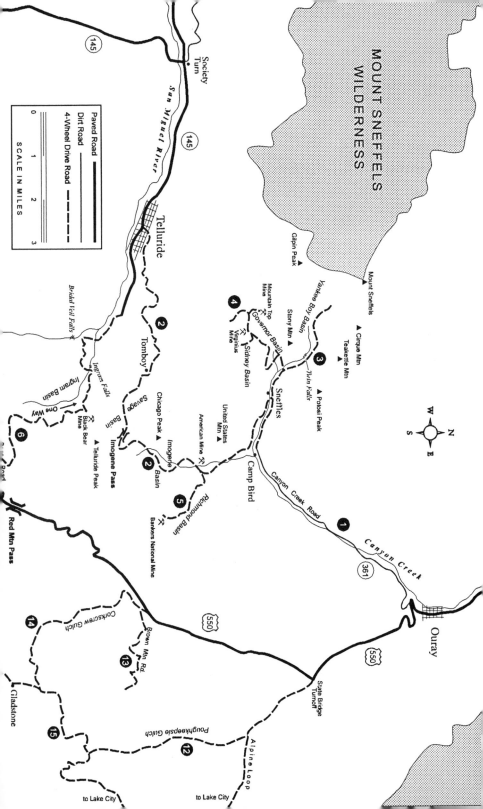

1. Canyon Creek Road

Trip Length: 2½ hours round trip to Sneffels from Ouray.

Difficulty Rating: #1–#2 on the lower route, #3 on the upper route.

High Point: 10,600 feet.

Maps: Text map p. 27; Uncompahgre National Forest; USGS: Ouray, Ironton; TI #141.

Route Variations: See Routes #2, #3, #4, and #5 for side routes or continuation to a destination.

Comments: A right turn off Highway 550 just south of Ouray will place you on County Road 361, a fairly smooth gravel road also known as the Canyon Creek Road. Built by Otto Mears as a supply road to the Camp Bird Mine, the road now passes through the highway department maintenance yard, past Box Canyon Falls, and continues as a gentle gravel road, at least for the first three miles. At approximately three miles United States Mountain looms ahead, where snowfields cover the shaded areas even in late summer.

As the road narrows the drop-offs increase, with 500- to 1,000-foot cliffs on the left and vertical walls on the right. Numerous waterfalls and wildflowers can be seen along the way. Historic sights in the area accesed by this route include the Camp Bird Mine, the town of Sneffels, the Virginius Mine, and Twin Falls which is better known in the advertising world as Coors Falls.

Route Directions: //From Ouray// Take Highway 550 south on Main Street in Ouray to a right turn onto County Road 361, approximately .7 mile from

The Canyon Creek Rd. and Canyon Creek.

the center of town. For the first three miles the road is a little bumpy with few drop-offs. At 3.7 miles the road becomes a narrow shelf road with steep drop-offs on the left, as it winds along the cliff wall. After a few curves and a little washboard, the road smooths out somewhat until you reach the hill right above the Camp Bird Mine at approximately 5 miles. Good driving skills are required as you climb the hill, especially in a 2-wheel drive vehicle, due to washout and ruts. At 6.2 miles the road becomes extremely narrow as you travel under overhanging cliffs, and conditions change with the road becoming fairly rough as you climb the hill. Good driving skills and higher clearance is recommended. When you reach 7 miles a left turn takes you to Imogene Basin and Imogene Pass (Route #2); a right turn takes you to Sneffels, where the buildings are nestled right in the cliffs and numerous mines dot the hills surrounding the townsite.

2. Imogene Pass (13,114 ft.)

Trip Length: 4 hours one way.

Difficulty Rating: #7–#8 at the higher locations, #4–#5 at the lower elevations.

High Point: 13,114 feet.

Maps: Text map p. 27; Uncompahgre National Forest; USGS: Ouray, Ironton, Telluride; TI #141.

Route Variations: See Routes #1, #3, #4, and #5 for side routes which offer spectacular beauty and points of historical interest. It is recommended that these side trips be explored separately if attempting to make a round trip from Ouray or Telluride in one day. Combine with Ophir Pass (Route #9) or with the Last Dollar Road (Route #7) for a round-trip route.

Comments: This route, which takes you through scenic valleys with pine forests and numerous waterfalls to the rugged terrain above timberline, is great for the intermediate 4-wheeler. Developed first as a mining trail and then as a maintenance road for the electrical power line from Ames, Colorado, to the Camp Bird Mine, the Imogene Pass Road displays not only scenic beauty, but historic splendor as you pass some of the best known mining camps of the late 1800s and early 1900s. The road starts out as a good gravel road, but turns into a narrow shelf road

Climbing to the top of Imogene Pass.

with several drop-offs and cliff overhangs. As you climb in altitude the road becomes rougher with several mud holes and stream crossings. However, views like the one of the Camp Bird Mill at the base of United States Mountain from the narrow road above, combined with the vast scenic views at the top of the pass, make this route a memorable experience.

Route Directions: //From Ouray// Take Highway 550 south on main street in Ouray to County Road 361, and follow the directions of Route #1 to the fork in the road just before Sneffels, where a left will take you into Imogene Basin and on to Imogene Pass. Follow the road as it winds around the base of United States Mountain, offering spectacular views of the Camp Bird Mill and the Canyon Creek Valley. Approximately 2.8 miles above the fork in the road, just before crossing Imogene Creek a second time, the road forks again. The left fork leads into Richmond Basin and the Bankers National Mine, the right fork continues through Imogene Basin to the narrow shelf road which will take you to the top of the Imogene Pass, the saddle at 13,114 feet between Telluride Peak and Chicago Peak.

As you start the final ascent to the saddle the road becomes very narrow, allowing only one vehicle to make the approach or descent at a time.

Approximately one-quarter mile from the top there is a difficult step requiring good technique and maneuverability in a limited space. After reaching the top begin the descent through the glacial cirque known as Savage Basin; here the road is a bit smoother than on the Imogene side. Descending through the basin you will encounter the Savage Basin Camp, better known as Tomboy for the Tomboy Mine located at 11,500 feet (about 3,000 feet above Telluride).

Continuing on from Tomboy the road winds down through a short tunnel into the San Miguel River Valley, with spectacular views to the south of Bridal Veil Falls, the switchbacks of Black Bear Pass, and on the southeast headwall—Ingram Falls. The ski slopes of Telluride and then the town appear as you continue to the valley floor.

//From Telluride// Follow Main Street to North Fir, go left to West Columbine. Turn left for one block to Oak Street where a right turn to the end of the street and another right will place you on the Imogene Pass Road. Follow the road over the pass and through Imogene Basin to the fork approximately 1 mile below the view of the Camp Bird Mill and Canyon Creek Valley. A right turn at the fork will lead you down Canyon Creek to Ouray; a left at the fork would take you into Governor and Yankee Boy basins.

3. Yankee Boy Basin

Trip Length: 3–3½ hours round trip from Ouray.

Difficulty Rating: #3–#4 at lower elevations, #7–#8 at upper elevations.

High Point: 12,600 feet.

Maps: Text map p. 27; Uncompahgre National Forest; USGS: Ouray, Ironton, Telluride; TI #141.

Route Variations: Combine with Route #1 from Ouray, or Route #2 from Telluride. For the best experience combine with Route #4 and/or Route #5 for a full day of exploration.

Comments: Above the Sneffels Township is a spectacular basin, one of the most historic mining districts of the San Juans, which is blanketed with every species of wildflower imaginable. As you pass through what is left of the Sneffels Township, Stony Mountain looms ahead with numerous mines and mining roads dotting the hillsides, giving evidence that this area was one of the highest gold producers in the entire country. The magnificent Yankee Boy Basin is surrounded by 13,000- and 14,000-foot jagged peaks, and a moonscape geography which is the home of pikas ("rock rabbits") and marmots. The numerous flowers along the route into Yankee Boy Basin include Indian Paint Brush, Aspen Daisy, Columbine, Cow Parsnip, and other varieties.

As the road becomes more challenging the scenery becomes even more spectacular as the Sneffels Range opens up in front and Twin Falls appears on the left. In late July or early August the meadows above the falls, blanketed with the many species of wildflowers, make this one of the prettiest alpine settings you will ever see. Higher in the basin the environment becomes harsher, and the delicate tundra and hearty wildflowers are the only vegetation to be found.

At the top of the basin are large moss rock fields, surrounded by the peaks of the Sneffels Range: Cirque Mountain (13,686 ft.), Potosi Peak (13,786 ft.), Teakettle Mountain (13,819 ft.), Gilpin Peak (13,694 ft.),and Mount Sneffels (14,150 ft.). You will know why this is known as the land of the pikas and marmots, as you see and hear their whistling sounds in the rocks above.

Twin Falls and the splendor of Yankee Boy Basin.

Route Directions: Make a right-hand turn at 7 miles above Ouray (see Route #1), and travel through the townsite of Sneffels in one-tenth of a mile. Stay to the right at 8.1 miles at the junction with the Governor Basin Road. The road is definitely 4-wheel drive from this point on. Twin Falls appears on the left, and the road becomes more difficult. At 9 miles the road splits with both roads converging two-tenths of a mile above; the upper road is the tougher of the two. Private land exists through this area, so stay on the designated road.

As you ascend above tree line, the road deteriorates rapidly. At 9.8 miles there is a pull-off with a trail leading to Wrights Lake, offering a nice hike for your enjoyment. The road turns into a #8 rating above this point, with loose rock and several rock steps that require good 4-wheel driving skills.

//From Telluride// Follow Route #2 to the top of Imogene Pass. At 5.4 miles down on the Ouray side make a left turn to the township of Sneffels and on to the Yankee Boy Basin Road, which will be a right turn at the fork with the Governor Basin Road.

4. Governor Basin

Trip Length: 3–3½ hours round trip from Ouray.

Difficulty Rating: #3–#4 at lower elevations, #6–#7 at upper elevations.

High Point: 12,800 feet.

Maps: Text map p. 27; Uncompahgre National Forest; USGS: Ouray, Ironton, Telluride; TI #141.

Route Variations: Combine with Routes #2, #3, and/or #5 for a full day of exploration.

Comments: One of the magnificent basins above the township of Sneffels is Governor Basin, situated between Yankee Boy to the north and Savage and Imogene basins to the southeast. The road which starts out easy, immediately starts climbing around the base of Stony Mountain via several switchbacks, giving you good views back into the Sneffels Valley and at the bottom of Yankee Boy Basin, Twin Falls, and the Sneffels Mountain Range.

As you climb steadily into the high basin the road narrows and is covered with loose shell rock, increasing difficulty to a #5–#6 difficulty rating. A

The intersection of Governor Basin Road and Yankee Boy Basin Road.

wide vehicle or one with very high clearance would have trouble negotiating this route due to trees which have fallen across the road limiting vehicle height. At the higher elevations there are great views of the Camp Bird Mine and Sneffels Township. Even in late August, wildflowers still cover the rolling alpine meadows created from the glacial activity that formed the lush basins below the ragged peaks.

History unfolds as you enter the area actually known as Governor Basin; the well-preserved Mountain Top Mine lies off to the right and other mines like the Virginius dot the jagged mountains around the basin. The main road through the basin is moderately difficult; however, several less traveled roads branch off toward the peaks and high alpine valleys. These roads are composed of loose gravel and rock, combined with a narrower path and slants which make travel very difficult. The difficult side trails branching off into other areas of the basin can catch an unaware explorer in an extremely difficult situation. Make sure you know the side route and what to expect before venturing into these uncharted trails without backup support.

Route Directions: Follow Route #1 to the township of Sneffels and continue on to the junction with the Yankee Boy Basin Road, approximately 8.1 miles from Ouray. Turn left for the road into Governor Basin. You start climbing rapidly from the valley floor with several switchback turns. At 1 mile there is a road to the right which is usually blocked by a gate (this road leads to a working mine), so stay to the left and continue climbing. As you reach the top of the hill the road is fairly rough, with loose rock and a fairly steep grade. Stay to the right following the well-traveled road as you climb.

When you have traveled 2 miles the road forks again, with the right fork continuing into Governor Basin and the left fork going over the hump into Sidney Basin, where after 1.8 miles it deadends among some old mines located below the jagged cliffs. Continuing on the right fork you will see the tailings of the Virginius Mine up to the left at nine-tenths of a mile. The road forks again with the right fork taking you to the Mountain Top Mine and the panoramic beauty of Governor Basin.

Roads crisscross the basin, but following the well-traveled route is easy. If you elect to explore some of the less traveled offshoots, make sure you are prepared for any situation.

//From Telluride// Follow Route #2 to the top of Imogene Pass. At 5.4 miles down the Ouray side make a left-hand turn to the township of Sneffels, and on to the Governor Basin turn on the left.

5. Richmond Basin

Trip Length: 3–3½ hours round trip trip from Ouray.

Difficulty Rating: #7–#8 at the upper elevations.

High Point: 12,600 feet.

Maps: Text map p. 27; Uncompahgre National Forest; USGS: Ouray, Ironton, Telluride; TI #141.

Route Variations: Combine with Routes #3 and #4 for a full day of exploration. Combine with Route #2 as a side trip on your way to Telluride or Ouray.

Comments: As you leave the road from Imogene Pass onto the Richmond Basin Road, you start climbing steadily past an old mine and through the pine forest on a moderately bumpy road. Approximately 1

A rocky descent down Richmond Basin Road.

mile above the road's beginning you break out of the forest into the huge rocky basin known as Richmond. Wetlands appear on the right-hand side as the road turns into a rocky shelf climbing steadily up and around the mountain's edge. The road deteriorates rapidly, reaching a #8 difficulty level, requiring the driver to maintain momentum to avoid getting stuck on the side of the mountain. You must use caution while negotiating this area since it is definitely a tire eater with sharp pointed rocks. Nothing but rocks and the remains of a miner's cabin can be seen as you look back from the bowl's rim onto the road you just traversed. The road deadends at a sheer drop-off and the Bankers National Mine, where remnants of the rich ore can be found in the mine tailings. The harsh environment with the magnificent views of the Sneffels Range gives you a hearty respect for the miners who worked these mines and developed this rugged road.

Route Directions: Follow Route #1 to the intersection with the Imogene Pass Road just before Sneffels, turn left on the Imogene Pass Road and follow it for a little over 2 miles where you cross Imogene Creek and the American Mine is ahead on the right-hand side. Continue on less than one-half of a mile to the intersection with the Richmond Basin Road and make a left. The road is very distinctive and provides no alternative routes like in Governor Basin. Climb steadily for 2.9 miles to the sheer cliff and the road's end.

//From Telluride// Follow Route #2 using the directions to the top of Imogene Pass. About 3 miles from the pass make a right turn onto the Richmond Basin Road.

6. Black Bear Road

Trip Length: 3–3½ hours one way from Ouray or Silverton to Telluride.

Difficulty Rating: #3–#4 for the first 10 miles; #8–#10 down into Telluride.

High Point: 12,900 feet.

Maps: Text map pp. 27, 42; Uncompahgre National Forest; San Juan National Forest; USGS: Ironton, Telluride; TI #141.

Route Variations: Combine this route with Route #2, #7, or #9 for a round trip from Ouray. Combine with Route #9 for the best round trip from Silverton.

Passing part of the Black Bear Mine on Black Bear Road.

Comments: This route is extremely deceiving and definitely not for the person with a fear of heights. At first Black Bear Road appears to be an easy route from the summit of Red Mountain Pass heading toward Telluride. As the road climbs into the high alpine meadows, a look back toward Red Mountain provides great views of the valley leading into Silverton and a good view of the Corkscrew Gulch Road. The road isn't extremely difficult as it travels through wide open meadows surrounded by towering cliffs and several waterfalls near the summit.

From the top you have views to the south of Red Mountain and the mountains surrounding Silverton, and to the north of the Sneffels Range and the mountains surrounding Telluride. Large meadows of tundra with small ponds greet you as you descend to the challenging part of Black Bear Road. Within a mile you are at Ingram Basin on a narrow shelf road circling the bowl at approximately 1,500 to 2,000 feet above the valley floor. This is not the most difficult part of the road, but it does get your attention and there is no turning back since it is one-way down the hill.

Continuing out of the bowl you get your first view of Telluride. The road becomes rougher as you make your descent, with several turns and larger rocks as you approach the remains of a mine. Just above the mine the road becomes a narrow shelf hugging the side of a cliff with 500-foot drops into the stream below. Rocks become steps and one mistake could be fatal; drive too fast and you'll know why this is "Pucker Point". Caution and common sense will get you through this difficult stretch and to the remains of the Black Bear Mine. However, you're not out of the woods yet. The road remains narrow as you hug the cliff with 2,000-foot drops and negotiate the hairpin, three-point turns down into Telluride.

Route Directions: //From Ouray// Follow Highway 550 south as it climbs toward the summit of Red Mountain Pass. At 13.8 miles, just after reaching the summit, Black Bear Road is on the right-hand side. As you climb up the road, stay to the right at the intersections. At 3.9 miles there is a split in the road where the right fork is shaded and can be covered by snow even in late summer; both forks join at the top of the hill. There are several different roads to choose from as you approach the top; the best and most traveled road is the one to the left. As you reach the top at 4.1 miles, the road to the top of the knoll gives you a great overview of the area, but it is a dead end. Stay to the left as you depart from the top on the more difficult side of Black Bear Road.

As you as you descend towards Telluride, there are few side roads and the main road is very evident. Once you get on the north side of Ingram Basin at 5.7 miles (a road on the right goes to a working mine) the road becomes one-way, open for downhill traffic only. At 5.8 miles three roads meet at the bottom of this small hill; the one to the right is the most traveled and should be considered the main road. From this point on the route is an obvious but very difficult road into Telluride.

//From Silverton// Follow Highway 550 north as it climbs the south side of Red Mountain Pass. At 9.5 miles, just before reaching the summit, Black Bear Road is on the left-hand side.

7. Last Dollar Road

Trip Length: 2–2½ hours one way.

Difficulty Rating: #2–#3.

High Point: 10,650 feet.

Maps: Text map p. 40; Uncompahgre National Forest; USGS: Telluride, Gray Head, Sams; TI #141.

Route Variations: Combine with Route #2, #6, or #9 for a round trip from Ouray or Telluride.

Comments: If you're heading north out of Telluride, this route offers an alternative to traveling the highway back to Ridgway, Ouray, or to other destinations. It is a nice country drive which will take you past the Telluride Airport and provide great views of Mount Wilson and the San Miguel River Valley. This road which winds through open meadows and across vast ranch lands was originally used as an early supply and mail route prior to Otto Mears' building the San Miguel Canyon Road, now the main route into Telluride from the north.

The road climbs through aspen and pine groves, past old cabins and evidence of sheep herder camps, until the Alder Creek/ Whipple Mountain Trailhead at the summit of the Last Dollar Road. The descent from the summit leads to vast open ranch lands as you break out of the forest onto Hastings Mesa, where many early homesteaders settled. Here they found the growing season too short for most crops, so they settled for cattle ranching or moved on.

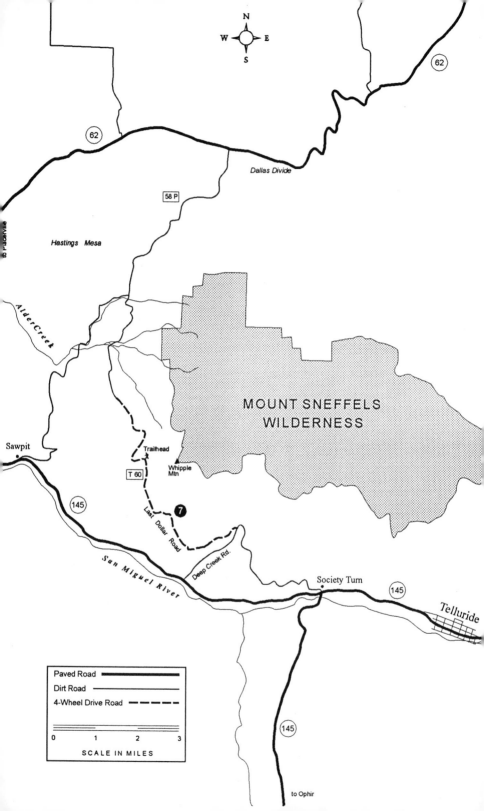

Route Directions: //From Telluride// Follow Highway 145 west from South Townsend Road for 3.2 miles to Society Turn for a right turn off the highway, at the Telluride Airport Road. Follow this road 1.9 miles to road T60, the Last Dollar Road. Six miles up the road is a great overlook to the left, as the road continues up to the right. At 8.5 miles take the left fork and the summit is only two-tenths of a mile ahead.

On the descent from the top there are several side roads; however, the main road is easy to follow. At 4.2 miles from the summit you cross Alder Creek, and in another 1.8 miles you are at the intersection of Last Dollar Road and County Road 58 P. Stay right to get to Highway 62 after another 5.2 miles of traveling across the high ranch plateau. Here, turning right takes you to Ridgway and Ouray, or turning left takes you to Placerville where a left puts you back on Highway 145 to Telluride.

//From Ridgway// Turn onto Highway 62 and travel 11.4 miles to the top of Dallas Divide; continue another 1.5 miles west and make a left on County Road 58 P. Travel 5.2 miles to a left onto County Road T 60, the Last Dollar Road. Follow the Last Dollar Road to Highway 145 where a left will take you into Telluride.

8. Alta and Alta Lakes Road

Trip Length: 2+ hours round trip from Telluride.

Difficulty Rating: #3 unless you take the right fork at the top, then you encounter #4 terrain.

High Point: 10,400 feet.

Maps: Text map p. 42; Uncompahgre National Forest; USGS: Telluride, Gray Head, Ophir; TI #141.

Route Variations: Combine with Routes #2, #6, #7, or #9 as a side trip.

Comments: When you're looking for a side trip, a picnic, fishing and camping, or just a short getaway, the road to Alta and Alta Lakes is a perfect choice within a short distance to Telluride. As you leave Highway 145 this narrow bumpy road climbs steadily through aspen and pine forests with beaver ponds. The old ghost town of Alta is well preserved with an old boarding house and numerous cabins. Views of the valley are spectacular as you travel above the ghost town to the lakes, where fishing and camping seem to be the pastime of choice. A side

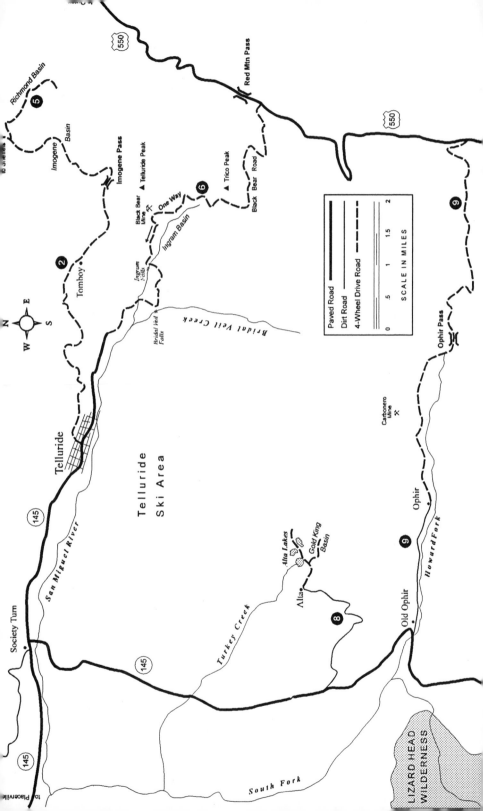

route off the Alta Lakes Road is a bit more difficult, but shows the resourcefulness of the early miners who would travel into every accessible valley in search of riches, as is evident by the mining works at the top of this high alpine basin. The views of Mount Wilson and Sunshine Mountain from this area are spectacular, and the resident marmots of Alta add to the character of this short jaunt.

Route Directions: From Telluride take the main road west 2.9 miles to the intersection of Highway 145 where a left puts you on the highway to Ophir and Rico. Take Highway 145 for 6.1 miles to the Alta Lakes Road on the left. Follow the narrow, bumpy road past the Alta Lakes Campground to the first cabins of Alta at 3.8 miles. Take the right fork past the ghost town to Alta Lakes where you encounter a fork in the road at six-tenths of a mile with the left fork taking you to the first of Alta Lakes, and camping. As you skirt the right side of the lake the road continues on to the east leading to the next lake in three-tenths of a mile, where the road deadends. The right fork takes you into a high alpine basin (Gold King Basin) and deadends at an old mine on the side of the basin at approximately 1 mile.

9. Ophir Pass (11,789 ft.)

Trip Length: 1¼ hours one way from Ophir to Highway 550.

Difficulty Rating: #5 as you climb to the pass on Ophir side; overall #4.

High Point: 11,789 feet.

Maps: Text map p. 42; San Juan National Forest, Uncompahgre National Forest; USGS: Ophir, Silverton; TI #141.

Route Variations: Combine with Routes #2, #6, or #7 as a round trip from Telluride to Ouray or Silverton.

Comments: This route which branches off from Highway 145 southwest of Telluride was once a major wagon toll road opened in 1881 to transport ore from Ophir (9,660 feet) over Ophir Pass to the processing mills in Silverton. By the mid 1880s, not only did Ophir have its own water works, electric lights and stamp mills, but it had 2 saloons, a newspaper, several stores, and a hotel. The road which originally put the town on the map heads east from main street into the rocky basin above timberline. Ophir Pass, a wider than normal mountain pass, lies at the top of the red rocky bowl. The road provides spectacular views of the valley around Ophir as it approaches the pass. The Silverton side of the Ophir Pass Road winds gently off the top through pine forests and open tundra meadows, where you have good views of waterfalls and two or three old mining works before connecting with Highway 550.

Route Directions: Follow the main road west from Telluride 2.9 miles to a left turn onto Highway 145 South. Go 7.7 miles to a left turn into Old Ophir. Another 2.2 miles further takes you to Ophir (New Ophir). Continue following the main road through Ophir towards Ophir Pass as it skirts the basin and breaks out over the pass 3.1 miles above town. The route on the other side of the pass is fairly easy and reaches Highway 550 in 4.4 miles from the summit, where a left on Highway 550 takes you back to Ouray or a right takes you into Silverton.

//From Ouray// Follow Highway 550 south to the summit of Red Mountain Pass. Continue 5.3 miles south from the summit to the Ophir Pass Road on your right. Follow the Ophir Pass Road over Ophir Pass and into Ophir, on to Highway 145 where a right turn will take you towards Telluride.

//From Silverton// Turn north on Highway 550 towards Red Mountain Pass and travel approximately 4.2 miles before making a left turn onto Ophir Pass Road.

The town of Ophir with Ophir Pass Road in the background.

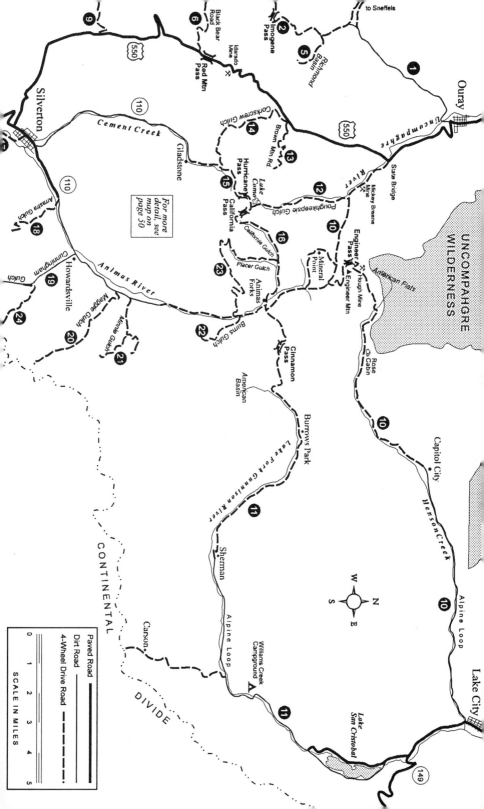

10. Engineer Pass (12,800ft.)

Trip Length: 4–4½ hours one way.

Difficulty Rating: #6–#7 on the Ouray side, #3 on the Lake City side.

High Point: 12,950 feet.

Maps: Text map p. 45; Uncompahgre National Forest, Gunnison National Forest; USGS: Ironton, Handies Peak, Red Cloud Peak, Uncompahgre Peak, Lake City; TI #141.

Route Variations: Combine with Route #11 to complete a round trip of the Alpine Loop. Combine with Routes #12 and #16 as a side trip or a difficult shortcut to Animas Forks.

Comments: Heading south from Ouray you will notice a large turnout to the left at the State Bridge with signs for the Alpine Loop. The road heading southeast from this point is the beginning of Engineer Pass Road. This early supply and stagecoach route was constructed by Otto Mears; the first stagecoach crossed the pass on August 10, 1877. Prior to leaving the turnout to follow this route, put your vehicle in low range, since you will begin rock climbing and technical maneuvering almost immediately. On the steady climb above Highway 550 through the pine and aspen forest, the narrow road hugs the canyon wall above the Uncompahgre River.

At approximately 1½ miles you will come upon the well-preserved buildings connected to the Mickey Breene Mine, which has been worked off and on into modern times. Continuing past the mine the road continues to climb over boulders and washed-out areas, past the turnoff to Poughkeepsie Gulch, to an open area just about tree line where the

town of Mineral Point once stood. Very little remains of this once prosperous mining camp which at one time had a post office, a store, a sawmill, restaurants, and saloons to serve the over 200 residents who lived at this 10,500-foot elevation.

The Alpine Loop sign at State Bridge.

As you travel above the open area and wind around 13,218-foot Engineer Mountain, the views of the San Juans are spectacular with the ultimate panoramic mountain view unfolding as you reach the top of the pass. Descending from the top of Engineer Pass on the Lake City side, the road winds through the gentle rolling grasslands and tundra known as American Flats. Further down in the basin next to the Frank Hough Mine was the location of Engineer City, known as the only city of its size without a saloon.

Engineer Pass Road.

Two miles further you will see the remains of the Rose Cabin, which was a country inn with sleeping rooms, a dining room, and bar. Rose Cabin was also an early stage stop where tired horses were exchanged for fresh ones for the journey over the pass to Ouray or Animas Forks. The road continues on through the remains of Capitol City, the only other town in Hinsdale County besides Lake City to be incorporated. The road improves considerably as it follows Henson Creek into Lake City.

Route Directions: //From Ouray// Follow Highway 550 south from Ouray for 4 miles to the State Bridge turnout. The road for Engineer Pass Road heads southeast from the turnout. At 2.6 miles, at the fork with Poughkeepsie Gulch Road, take the left fork to continue up Engineer Pass Road. You will encounter the open area where Mineral Point was located 3.9 miles above the Poughkeepsie Gulch intersection. In another mile, at the fork, take a left to continue over Engineer Pass; the right fork is a cutoff to Animas Forks. At 2.4 miles above this fork is the top of the pass. The road from the top of the pass on the Lake City side is easy to follow for the remaining 12.5 miles to Lake City.

//From Lake City// Follow Second Street west and continue on the maintained gravel road along Henson Creek. The summit of Engineer Pass is 12.5 miles from town. Descending to Ouray take the right fork at 2.4 miles from the top, and another right at the Poughkeepsie intersection 4.9 miles further down. At 2.6 miles from this intersection the road meets Highway 550, where a right turn takes you to Ouray in 4.0 miles.

11. Cinnamon Pass (12,640 ft.)

Trip Length: 4–4½ hours one way Lake City to Ouray. 3–3½ hours one way Lake City to Silverton.

Difficulty Rating: #5–#6 as you approach the summit on Lake City side.

High Point: 12,640 feet.

Maps: Text map p. 45; Gunnison National Forest, Uncompahgre National Forest; USGS: Ironton, Handies Peak, Redcloud Peak, Lake San Cristobal; TI #141.

Route Variations: Combine with Route #10 to complete the Alpine Loop. Combine with Routes #16/#12, or Routes #16/#15/#14 for alternate routes back to Ouray.

Comments: Not another road in the San Juans or possibly in the state of Colorado offers the beauty and serenity of the Cinnamon Pass Road. Heading south from Lake City along the Lake Fork of the Gunnison River, past Lake San Cristobal (the largest natural body of water in the state of Colorado), this fairly well-maintained road leads to the lush rolling hills of grass and tundra that welcome you on the way to the top of the pass. Originally a well-traveled Indian trail, this route became one of the most important pioneer roads of the area, connecting the supply area of Lake City with the mining camps surrounding Animas Forks and Silverton. The remains of Burrows Park (also known as Whitecross) and several other small mining communities mark the way before the narrow shelf road which climbs to the top. During the height of summer the rolling alpine meadows seem to be covered with what appears to be white rocks from a distance; however, as one gets closer, the rocks seem to move and turn into large flocks of sheep grazing on the lush high alpine grass. From the top of Cinnamon Pass the road smooths out again and rapidly descends into the upper canyons of the Animas River to the well-preserved ghost town of Animas Forks.

Coming down from Cinnamon Pass into Animas Forks.

Route Directions: //From Lake City// Follow Highway 149 south from Lake City for 2.3 miles to the Lake San Cristobal turnoff. Continue around the lake on the paved road; 4 miles from the turnoff, just beyond the far end of the lake, the pavement ends and the road becomes a maintained gravel road. Almost 3 miles past the lake is the Williams Creek Campground and 2 miles past the campground is a difficult 4-wheel drive road on the left which leads to the ghost town of Carson located near the top of the Continental Divide.

About 8 miles past the Carson turnoff you will travel through the remains of the ghost town of Burrows Park. After another 3 miles you will pass the American Basin intersection and climb the final two miles on a rougher road up to Cinnamon Pass.

Descending into the Animas River Valley you will encounter a fork at 1.5 miles where you can stay right either to continue on the Alpine Loop to Engineer Pass, or to take the shortest route to Ouray. Staying left at this junction will take you down to Animas Forks. At Animas Forks a left turn takes you into Silverton. A right at Animas Forks will take you over California Pass (Route #16) and gives you several alternatives for a trip to Ouray.

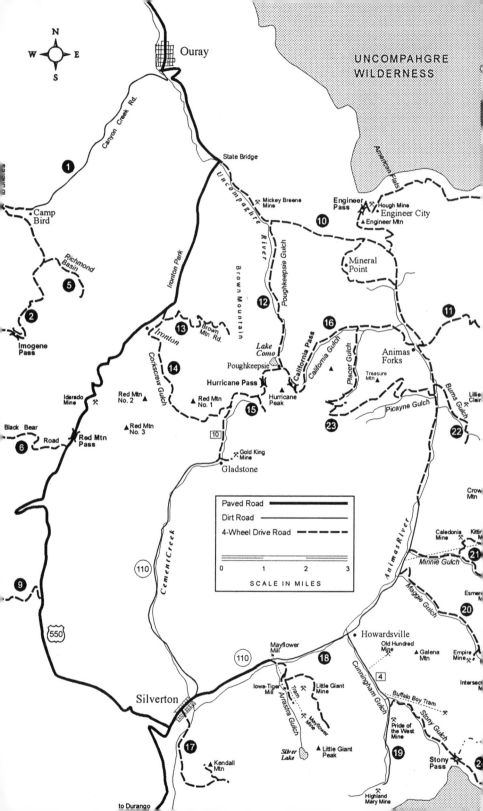

Trouble at the "Wall" in Poughkeepsie Gulch.

12. Poughkeepsie Gulch

Trip Length: 1½ hours as a side trip from Engineer Pass. 3–3½ hours to Silverton.

Difficulty Rating: #7–#8 overall, #10 at the Wall.

High Point: 12,900 feet.

Maps: Text map pp. 50, 45; Uncompahgre National Forest; USGS: Ironton, Handies Peak; TI #141.

Route Variations: Combine with Route #10 as a side trip, with Routes #14/#15, or #16 for a trip to Silverton or a round trip to Ouray.

Comments: This short but difficult route will challenge even the most experienced 4-wheeler. After leaving the Engineer Pass Road, you first think this side road is going to be easy as you travel through the pine forest and through several mud holes. However, as you ascend into the gulch the road changes into loose shell rock until you reach the "Wall". The Wall is a large rock formation where the road seems to disappear. There are three ways to continue: to the left through the mud you can skirt the obstacle; climbing the obstacle on the right hand side is the most difficult route and requires modified equipment; or climbing the left side of the obstacle is slightly easier, but still extremely challenging. Only a few stock vehicles are capable of overcoming this obstacle by themselves, which is why the road is considered a dead end. If you are one of the fortunate ones to make it past the obstacle, you can continue on to Lake Como with a choice of either taking California Pass (Route #16) or Hurricane Pass (Route #15) into Silverton.

Route Directions: From Ouray travel 4.0 miles south on Highway 550 to State Bridge and the Engineer Pass Road turnoff on the left. Follow the Engineer Pass Road for 2.6 miles to a right onto the Poughkeepsie Gulch Road. Follow the road through the gulch, staying to the right at all intersections until you reach the Wall. Most stock vehicles will need to turn around at this point and return to Engineer Pass Road. If you are able to conquer the Wall, continue out of the gulch to Lake Como and the remains of Poughkeepsie townsite, where a right will take you over Hurricane Pass (Route #15) and a left over California Pass (Route #16).

//From Silverton// Follow County Road 110 from Silverton to Animas Forks. Continue following Route #16 over California Pass; at the bottom of the pass continue to the right down Poughkeepsie Gulch until you reach Engineer Pass Road where a left will take you to Highway 550 and Ouray (north) or Silverton (south).

Part of the Idarado Mine Complex.

13. Brown Mountain Road

Trip Length: 2 hours round trip.

Difficulty Rating: #3–#4 until you reach the top; #9–#10 on upper road.

High Point: 11,850 feet.

Maps: Text map pp. 50, 45; Uncompahgre National Forest; USGS: Ironton; TI #141.

Route Variations: Combine as a side trip with Corkscrew Gulch Road (Route #14).

Comments: Brown Mountain is just north of Red Mountain #1. Splitting from the Corkscrew Gulch Road near Highway 550, Brown Mountain Road leads through heavily forested areas past an area which still has a couple buildings standing with old mining equipment. Further on the forest opens up providing spectacular views of the mining activities below, Red Mountain, and the Black Bear Road (Route #6). At tree line you encounter a wetlands area with a small pond surrounded by a high alpine meadow. Higher up the route continues on a narrow shelf crossing a steep rock field where the road is off canter and becomes extremely difficult. The ride up Brown Mountain is a superb side trip offering great picnic points with a view, and some technical 4-wheeling.

Route Directions: Take Highway 550 south from Ouray to the flat Ironton Park area before the ascent to the Idarado Mine. At 1.6 miles past mile marker 88 make a left-hand turn. Continue around the mine tailings approximately one-half mile and take the left fork. At 1.8 miles you encounter the mining remains, and in another 1.7 miles you break above timberline. The road becomes extremely narrow and rough within one-half mile and deadends within another half mile near the rock slide area.

//From Silverton// Follow Route #14 to the valley on the Red Mountain side. As the road leaves the forest and enters the mines area, a road intersects to the right. This road will take you up Brown Mountain.

The author at the junction of Brown Mountain Rd. and Corkscrew Gulch Rd.

14. Corkscrew Gulch Road

Trip Length: 1½–2 hours.

Difficulty Rating: #5 under normal conditions, could increase in difficulty with bad weather.

High Point: 12,217 feet.

Maps: Text map pp. 50, 45; Uncompahgre National Forest; USGS: Ironton; TI #141.

Route Variations: Combine with the side trip up Brown Mountain (Route #13), or with Routes #15/#16 to reach Animas Forks.

Comments: The Corkscrew Gulch Road is a shortcut over the Red Mountains from the ghost town of Ironton to Cement Creek and Gladstone. Cut out of the mountain to move drilling equipment into the area in recent years, this route travels across fields of yellow clay which could make for extremely difficult driving under wet conditions. As you travel through pine and aspen forests to red rock at the base of Red Mountain you will see breathtaking views of the Red Mountains, which continually change under varying light conditions. The hairpin turns winding to the top will remind you why this is called Corkscrew Gulch. At the saddle between Red Mountain #1 and Red Mountain #2 you're above the tundra on red rock, where the wind seems to blow continually. On the descent from the top into the Cement Creek Basin you see mining activity, with the Gladstone area to the south, and the basin below Hurricane Mountain and Hurricane Pass to the north. During mid to late summer beautiful wildflowers line the route, providing a spectacular contrast with the mineral-rich red slopes that surround this area.

Route Directions: //From Silverton// Take County Road 110 northeast from town for approximately one-half mile to a left turn on County Road 110 to Gladstone. At the Gladstone townsite the road splits. The right fork goes into the mine area; the left fork (County Road 10) continues around the mine toward the Corkscrew Gulch Road. At 1.6 miles from Gladstone, turn left onto the Corkscrew Gulch Road. Follow this road for just over a mile to the saddle at the top, from where a winding descent will take you to Highway 550 in another 3 miles. At Highway 550 a left turn will take you over Red Mountain Pass back to Silverton, or a right will take you into Ouray.

//From Ouray// Follow Highway 550 south from town up toward Red Mountain Pass. At 1.6 miles past mile marker 88 make a left-hand turn just before the mine tailings from the mines at the ghost town of Ironton. As you enter the pine forest take the right fork and continue climbing up around the slopes of the Red Mountains to the saddle 3 miles from the bottom. Continue down from the saddle for a little over a mile to intersect County Road 10. A right turn will take you past Gladstone into Silverton and a left will take you over Hurricane Pass (Route #15).

15. Hurricane Pass (12,407 ft.)

Trip Length: 1½ hours to Lake Como from Silverton; 3½ hours or more when combined with alternate routes.

Difficulty Rating: #5–#6.

High Point: 12,407 feet.

Maps: Text map pp. 50, 45; Uncompahgre National Forest; USGS: Ironton, Handies Peak; TI #141.

Route Variations: Combine with Route #16 for a round trip from Silverton. Combine with Routes #16 (or #12) and #14 as a round trip from Ouray.

Comments: The hills above Gladstone are covered with remnants of the mining activities dating back to the 1870s, with evidence of the booming mining camps in the valleys below the mountain peaks. Hurricane Pass Road was established to connect two of these camps, Gladstone and Poughkeepsie, and to serve as a supply corridor for the mines dotting the hillsides.

From Gladstone the road climbs steadily through the pine forest to the intersection with Corkscrew Gulch Road. Above this intersection the area opens into a wide open basin with evidence of mineral deposits, great rock formations, and a waterfall at the head of the basin. The road skirts the left side of the basin, passes the remains of the Queen Anne Mine, and begins to deteriorate a bit more as it climbs through the wide open rocky basin, covered occasionally by sparse tundra.

At the brown and barren top of Hurricane Pass (12,407 feet) is a pull-out on the left which will give you a great view of Lake Como and the area where the mining camp of Poughkeepsie once stood. Poughkeepsie, like many mining camps, had a store, restaurants, a couple saloons, and a summer population of approximately 250. The population dwindled to only a few hardy soles in winter since this was one of the highest mining camps in the San Juans. During heavy snow years there is typically a snow wall along the road on the Poughkeepsie side, even into late summer. Descending down the short distance from the top of the pass to the basin next to Lake Como the road is fairly rocky but not extremely difficult.

The intersection of the roads to Poughkeepsie Gulch, Hurricane Pass, and California Pass by Lake Como at the site of Poughkeepsie.

Route Directions: //From Silverton// Follow Highway 110 northeast and in one-half mile take the left fork on County Road 110 to Gladstone. At Gladstone take the left fork onto County Road 10 and follow this road through the pine forest. At 1.6 miles above Gladstone County Road 10 intersects the Corkscrew Gulch Road (Route #14) where you stay right and continue into the wide open basin. After passing the Queen Anne Mine the road forks 1.2 miles above the Corkscrew Road intersection. The left fork is the way to the top, while the right fork deadends after eight-tenths of a mile in a rocky area at an altitude of 12,361 feet. This offshoot does give you a great view of Corkscrew Gulch Road, the road you just traveled, and the valley below.

The top of Hurricane Pass is just six-tenths of a mile above the road fork. From the top of the pass it is only one-half mile to several intersecting roads and the open area where Poughkeepsie once stood. A left turn will take you down the difficult Poughkeepsie Gulch Road (Route #12) to the intersection with Engineer Pass Road (Route #10), and a right will take you over California Pass (Route #16) to Animas Forks.

16. California Pass (12,930 ft.)

Trip Length: 1¾ hours one way from Silverton to Lake Como. 3½ hours or more when combined with route variations.

Difficulty Rating: #5 at the most difficult points.

High Point: 12,930 feet.

Maps: Text map pp. 50, 45; Uncompahgre National Forest; USGS: Handies Peak; TI #141.

Route Variations: Combine with Routes #15 and #14 for a long round trip to Silverton. Combine with Route #12 and the bottom of Route #10 for a one-way trip to Ouray.

Comments: As you head west from Animas Forks you're entering into possibly the richest gold-producing gulch of the San Juans. The wide open basin is dotted with mines—the early miners filed claims one right after the other. Climbing up the right hand side of the basin you travel past a well-preserved mine that has held up to the harsh winters. Further on the basin opens into lush meadows of high alpine tundra below the red rock slopes that line the top where California Pass provided a short route from Poughkeepsie to Animas Forks. From the turnout at the pass a short walk to the highest point provides a spectacular view of Lake Como to the north, and a great overview of California Gulch.

Route Directions: //From Silverton// Follow Road 110 northeast from Silverton along the Animas River for 12.5 miles to the ghost town of Animas Forks. Here three roads converge on the town; take the one furthest left leading into California Gulch. At 1.3 miles past Animas Forks stay right at the intersection with Placer Gulch, and continue up on the right side of the basin until reaching California Pass 3 miles ahead. After a descent of nine-tenths of a mile, you reach the area of the former encampment of Poughkeepsie, and the intersection with the Hurricane Pass Road (Route #15) and the Poughkeepsie Gulch Road (Route #12).

//From Ouray// Follow Route #12 or Routes #14/#15 to Lake Como and the intersection. The road furthest left will take you over California Pass, through California Gulch to Animas Forks. Make sure to stay left at the Placer Gulch intersection 3 miles down from California Pass. Continue on Road 110 south along the Animas River for 12.5 miles into Silverton.

17. Kendall Mountain Road

Trip Length: 2¾ hours round trip.

Difficulty Rating: #6–#8 overall, with areas of #9 and #10 on spurs at the top.

High Point: 12,763 feet.

Maps: Text map p. 50; San Juan National Forest; USGS: Silverton, Howardsville; TI #141.

Route Variations: Combine with Routes #18, #19, #20, or #21 for a full day of exploration.

Comments: Kendall Mountain rises to the south of Silverton; the road that winds around the back of the mountain provides a challenging drive combined with panoramic views. This road is not maintained, as you soon find out after crossing the Animas River and starting around the north face of the mountain. As the road turns to the south side, the main ascent begins. On the steady climb through the forest you occasionally get a glimpse of the surrounding valleys south to Durango and the Highway 550 corridor.

There is little evidence of mining until you climb above timberline into the rocky basin on the opposite side of the mountain from Silverton. The road becomes more difficult as it ascends above the forest floor into the tundra-covered basin which shortly gives way to a rocky moonscape setting with rock spires and black rock. It is clear as you look at the basin that it was formed during the ice ages, as the rocks seem to be

Kendall Mountain Road on a wintry day.

strategically placed and the back bowl perfectly formed. With the narrow roads and steep slopes at the top of the basin you could find yourself in a very difficult situation should bad weather move in. On the mountain's south side a couple of side roads give you the chance to explore the rocky cliffs or drive to a scenic overlook of Silverton and Highway 550 climbing up Red Mountain Pass.

Route Directions: Head east on Main Street to Fourteenth Street where a right turn will take you to the Kendall Mountain Road. After crossing the Animas River turn right again and start climbing up Kendall Mountain. The road winds around to the south side of the mountain through the forest to a wide open basin above timberline. At 5.7 miles there is a fork in the road and a mine which is closed off by a wire gate. The right fork will take you into the rocky basin that resembles a moonscape. In half a mile, at a second fork, staying left will take you to a dead end at the base of the rock spires in two-tenths of a mile. Taking the right fork is very precarious, with the road turning into a level #10 which should not be attempted without proper equipment and a second vehicle.

At the closed-off mine the left fork heads northwest past a weather observation station/radio transmitter at 1 mile from the fork. In another two-tenths of a mile is a turnaround spot which should be considered the end of the road. You can walk another one-tenth of a mile to a birds-eye view of Silverton and the surrounding valleys. You will need to backtrack to return to Silverton.

18. Arrastra Gulch

Trip Length: 1½ hours or more depending on side routes and trails explored.

Difficulty Rating: #2–#3 below Iowa-Tiger Mill side road, #5–#6 above the road.

High Point: 11,600 feet.

Maps: Text map p. 50; San Juan National Forest; USGS: Howardsville; TI #141.

Route Variations: Combine with Routes #17, #19, #20, #21, or #22 for a full day of exploration.

The Mayflower Tram.

Comments: The road into Arrastra Gulch is short, but takes you up possibly the most historic gulch in the area. Several mines and processing mills can be seen as you travel up the gulch, along with the remains of several tram lines, including the one from the Mayflower Mine which still spans Highway 110 just before the Mayflower Mill. At the top of the gulch is the Little Giant Mine (founded in 1870), noted as the first successful mine claim and operation in the Silverton area. It was at the Little Giant where an arrastra was first used to process the ore, an arrastra being a large round stone turned by a donkey or mule to crush the ore. Hence the name Arrastra Gulch. The many tram lines that crisscross the gulch transported ore from mines high on the basin walls to the mills located at the base of the gulch.

As you follow the main Arrastra Gulch Road it opens up into a high alpine meadow where remnants of the old mills can be seen next to the creek below. Soon the concrete bases of the Silver Lake Tram can be seen as the meadow opens on the right-hand side. Above the secondary road leading to the Iowa-Tiger Mill the road becomes more difficult, turning to loose shelly rock. Traversing the slopes of Little Giant Peak further up, the road crosses another rocky area and ends at a wide parking/turnaround area. Several hiking trails depart from this area and lead to the mines above.

Route Directions: Follow Highway 110 northeast from Silverton for 2.1 miles to just before the Mayflower Mill on the left and the Mayflower Tram Line. Take the right turn down the hill and continue across the Animas River into the gulch. At five-tenths of a mile stay left and continue up the gulch as a side road on the right leads to the Aspen Mine. Stay left again a mile further where another road on the right leads to the site of the Iowa-Tiger Mill. Within one-half mile a road leading to the left takes you to Little Giant Basin and above the Little Giant Mine. Staying right will take you to the end of the main road in a little over 1 mile, where you will need to turn around and backtrack to Highway 110.

19. Cunningham Gulch

Trip Length: 2½ hours.

Difficulty Rating: #5 toward the top of the gulch.

High Point: 10,500 feet.

Maps: Text map p. 50; San Juan National Forest; USGS: Howardsville; TI #141.

Route Variations: Combine with Routes #17, #18, #20, #21, #22 or #23 for further exploration. Combine with Route #24 for a full day venture.

Comments: This gulch just northeast of Arrastra is also historic; however, it is more hands-on, with the opportunity to actually explore an old mine, via the Old Hundred Mine Tour. At the junction of Highway 110 and Cunningham Gulch are the remains of Howardsville, the most important settlement in the area during the 1870s. Howardsville became the commercial center for the entire area due to its location at the end of the shortest supply route into the valley from the Del Norte area and the San Luis Valley.

As you follow the gulch past the Old Hundred Mill and Mine, the valley floor is wide open with unobstructed views of the timber-lined slopes rising above the valley floor, where beaver ponds and old-style corrals provide signs of inhabitants past and present. Just before the road starts steadily climbing to the end of the gulch is the intersection with the Stony Pass Road (Route #24); the road up the gulch becomes slightly more difficult from this point on. Continuing up the gulch you will pass evidence of the Pride of the West Mine on the left and several areas where snowslide activity occurs during the winter months, including the Pride of the West slide area, known as one of the most destructive slide areas in the valley.

As the road climbs along the left side of the valley it steadily deteriorates, turning into a narrow shelly road that eventually

The mine at the top of Cunningham Gulch.

deadends at the unobstructed opening of an old mine which possibly connects to the Highland Mary Mine. Old mines of this type should not be entered by amateurs since they may contain deadly gases which are undetectable, along with other inherent dangers which place an inexperienced explorer at risk.

Route Directions: Follow Highway 110 northeast from Silverton for 4.2 miles to the intersection with County Road 4 at Howardsville; make a right-hand turn onto Cunningham Gulch Road. The Old Hundred Mine Tour is on the left approximately 1 mile from the intersection. At 2 miles from Howardsville, Stony Pass Road goes off to the left. Continue right at this intersection along the left side of the valley, across the stream to a dead end at the mine. Backtrack to the Stony Pass Road or to Highway 110.

20. Maggie Gulch

Trip Length: 2½ hours.

Difficulty Rating: #5 toward the top of the gulch.

High Point: 11,800 feet.

Maps: Text map p. 50; San Juan National Forest, Rio Grande National Forest, Gunnison National Forest, Uncompahgre National Forest; USGS: Howardsville; TI #141.

Route Variations: Combine with Routes #17, #18, #19, #21, #22, or #23 for an exciting day of exploring.

Comments: Follow Highway 110 past the Cunningham Gulch turn (Route #19) for a short distance around the base of Galena Mountain and you will see Maggie Gulch on the right side. Turn onto the Maggie Gulch Road and you will immediately start climbing through the thick pine forest which lines the gulch. As you gain altitude and break out of the trees the gulch opens up to a box canyon on the right side with a spectacular waterfall plummeting at least 1,000 feet, and a narrow road which skirts a large rock field on the left. Once you pass the rock field you climb above the box canyon to a lush green valley where the road runs along the right-hand side with the creek 500 feet below. Toward the top of the valley the road becomes a bit more difficult as it reaches a wide open basin covered with high alpine grass and tundra. You pass a side road to the Empire Mine as you climb to the top of the basin where the road deadends at the remains of the Intersection Mine and Mill. During the late summer months it is possible to encounter large herds of sheep grazing these high alpine meadows.

Route Directions: Head northeast on Highway 110 from Silverton for 6.3 miles to the turnoff on the right to Maggie Gulch Road. Immediately make a left turn after the outhouse and start climbing through the pine forest (the road to the right travels into the trees where two nice campsites are located). You will break out of the trees approximately 1 mile from the bottom with the box canyon view. At 4 miles the road forks with the right fork continuing approximately 1 mile to the Empire Mine and the left fork continuing to the top of the gulch and the Intersection Mine and Mill. Turn around and backtrack to Highway 110.

21. Minnie Gulch

Trip Length: 2 hours.

Difficulty Rating: #5 at the most difficult points.

High Point: 11,600 feet.

Maps: Text map p. 50; San Juan National Forest, Gunnison National Forest, Rio Grande National Forest, Uncompahgre National Forest; USGS: Howardsville; TI #141.

Route Variations: Combine with Routes #18, #19, #20, #22, or #23 for more exploration.

Comments: If you follow Highway 110 northeast past the turnoffs to Arrastra, Cunningham, and Maggie gulches you will reach the Minnie Gulch Road. The road climbs above Minnie Creek and is very narrow with drop-offs on the right and steep inclines on the left until it climbs into a thick pine forest. After crossing Minnie Creek you can look back and see a large concrete structure—the remains of the Caledonia Mill. Within a short distance you will see the remains of a couple buildings on the left, including the Caledonia Mill Boarding House. A short distance further you will see remnants of the Kittimac Tram just before crossing

An unexpected obstacle on the Minnie Gulch Road.

Minnie Creek again. After the creek crossing the road forks; the left fork goes to the Kittimac Mine and the right continues up the gulch to the Esmerelda Mine.

The left fork of the road winds into a large basin and passes more structures which are the remains of the Caledonia Mine Boarding House and several cabins, all that have withstood time and the tough San Juan winters. As you climb above timber-line the road skirts Crown Mountain to end at the Kittimac Mine. Most of the structure at this point has collapsed; however, you can get a good perspective of the mine and experience a great view of the valley below.

If you follow the right fork of the Minnie Gulch Road up the gulch, it will lead to the Esmerelda Mine which produced large shipments of gold and silver around the turn of the century.

Route Directions: Head northeast on Highway 110 toward Animas Forks to the Minnie Gulch Road 7.4 miles from Silverton. Turn right and follow the road up to the left as it climbs above Minnie Creek. Continue up the road approximately 3 miles where it forks with the left fork going to the Kittimac Mine and the right fork leading to the Esmerelda Mine. The left fork deadends at the mine within nine-tenths of a mile; the right fork deadends at the Esmerelda Mine 1.25 miles above the intersection. Backtrack this route to Highway 110.

22. Burns Gulch

Trip Length: 1½ hours.

Difficulty Rating: #5.

High Point: 11,900 feet.

Maps: Text map p. 50; San Juan National Forest, Gunnison National Forest, Uncompahgre National Forest; USGS: Handies Peak; TI #141.

Route Variations: Combine with Routes #18, #19, #20, #21, or #23 for further exploration.

Comments: Burns Gulch is the last gulch on the right before Animas Forks when following Highway 110 from Silverton. The Burns Gulch Road turns right across the Animas River just after the left turn to Picayne Gulch (Route #23). As you climb above the trees into the basin you will notice remnants of mining activity on both hillsides above the gulch. High on the left are the mine dumps from the Lillie Claim which was discovered in 1873, becoming the first claim in Burns Gulch. Those on the right across the stream are from the La Plata Grande and Great Eastern claims. From the top of the gulch you have an overview of the mining activity and exploration which continued in the gulch along Burns Creek into the 1950s.

Route Directions: Follow Highway 110 for 9.5 miles northeast toward Animas Forks. Just past the Picayne Gulch turnoff on the left, turn right and ford the Animas River. During high water months continue about 100 yards across the bridge, then turn right and double back to the Burns Gulch Road. Continue climbing up the road approximately 2 miles where it intersects with a short spur to the right, which is very difficult and deadends. Stay left following the switchback turns to an open area where you cross Burns Creek and the road deadends. Two hiking trails can be followed from the road's end if desired.

23. Picayne and Placer Gulches

Trip Length: 2½ hours.

Difficulty Rating: #5.

High Point: 12,750 feet.

Maps: Text map p. 50; Uncompahgre National Forest, Gunnison National Forest; USGS: Handies Peak; TI #141

Route Variations: Combine with Routes #20, #21, or #22 for a full day in the Animas Forks area.. Combine with Route #16/#12 to continue on to Ouray, or Route #16/#15 for a round trip to Silverton.

Comments: If you follow the Animas River Valley northeast from Silverton you will reach the turnoff for Picayne Gulch just before Animas Forks. On the climb up the open slopes at the base of the gulch you have a spectacular view of the Animas River Valley and the high peaks rising above the valley floor. You pass a few mine dumps as you circle behind Treasure Mountain through the high alpine meadows, where wildflowers abound from mid July into August, to a pine and aspen forest. As the road switchbacks up the mountain, old mining cabins which have withstood the severe winters of the area appear on the left. Above the mine camp in the open basin are remnants of several mines which were worked by the camp's inhabitants.

Picayne Gulch gets an early winter.

The road continues to climb entering another group of pine trees before breaking into another meadow where it connects with the Placer Gulch Road. As you climb over the tundra-covered ridge and descend into Placer Gulch the slopes become rockier with little vegetation and evidence of more mining activity. As you drop to the base of Placer Gulch you get good views of California Gulch.

Route Directions: Follow Highway 110 northeast of Silverton towards Animas Forks for 9.4 miles, where you make a left turn onto Picayne Gulch Road. Climb 3.9 miles up the gulch, past the mining camp below the Toltec Mine, where the road forks. Take the left fork for the climb over the ridge into Placer Gulch, where it will intersect with the California Gulch Road approximately 2.8 miles below. A right turn will take you to Animas Forks and complete this loop; a left turn will take you over California Pass to Poughkeepsie Gulch (Route #12) or Hurricane Pass (Route #15).

24. Stony Pass (12,590 ft.)

Trip Length: 4½ hours one way.

Difficulty Rating: #4.

High Point: 12,590 feet.

Maps: Text map pp. 50, 69; Rio Grande National Forest, San Juan National Forest; USGS: Howardsville, Pole Creek Mountain, Rio Grande Pyramid; TI #141, #140.

Route Variations: Combine with Route #25 for a full day of exploring. Combine with Route #11 for a round trip to Silverton.

Comments: The road over Stony Pass was the shortest supply route to the Animas River Valley from Del Norte and the San Luis Valley in the 1870s and early 1880s. However, its use declined in 1882 after the Denver and Rio Grand Railroad reached Silverton. Not only was this the first wagon road into the Animas River Valley, but also the first route taken by an automobile into the area in 1910. Today it is a gentle mountain pass road which climbs along the side of Stony Mountain, past the Buffalo Boy Tram to the Continental Divide.

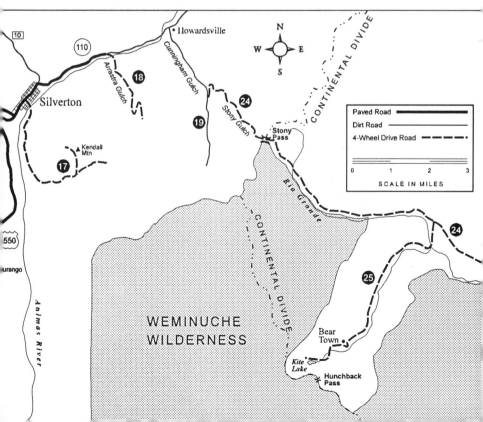

View from the ascent of Stony Pass Road.

After you climb from the beaver ponds at the base of the route through the thick pine forest to the wide open meadows surrounded by jagged red rocks, you will encounter breathtaking panoramic views of the southern San Juans from the top of the Divide. As you cross Stony Pass into the wide open meadow and into the Rio Grande Drainage, you will pass an old building at the Summit Mine. The road continues to drop through the open tundra, skirts the forest area of the Weminuche Wilderness, and passes the Rio Grande Reservoir where civilization is seen once again. From here the route continues through the rolling valleys that follow the beginnings of the Rio Grande River.

Route Directions: Follow Highway 110 northeast of Silverton 4.2 miles to Howardsville and turn right at the intersection with County Road 4 (Route #19). Continue 2 miles on County Road 4 where the Stony Pass Road, County Road 3, intersects; turn left and follow the Stony Pass Road over the Continental Divide, staying left at all intersections. Follow the gravel road which skirts the left side of Rio Grande Reservoir onto pavement and to the intersection with Highway 149 where a left will take you back over Slumgullion Pass into Lake City, or a right will take you to Creede.

25. Bear Town and Kite Lake

Trip Length: 2 hours.

Difficulty Rating: #6 at the top.

High Point: 12,100 feet.

Maps: Text map p. 69; Rio Grande National Forest, San Juan National Forest; USGS: Pole Creek Mountain, Rio Grande Pyramid, Storm King Peak; TI #141, #140.

Route Variations: Combine with Route #24 as a side trip.

Comments: Making a right turn off the Stony Pass Road to Kite Lake is a side trip well worth your time. After crossing the headwaters of the Rio Grande, you travel through the high alpine meadows used as summer pasture for cattle, and climb through the open valley past the site of Bear Town, a former gold mining town, to the peaceful setting of Kite Lake. The last two miles before the lake can become very difficult with stretches of loose talus rock. Traveling around the lake to the foot of the rocky cliffs takes you to a spectacular view of the valleys below. Anyone interested in hiking will find the trailhead for Hunchback Pass at this point. The trail goes above the lake, over the pass, and into the Weminuche Wilderness.

Route Directions: Follow Route #24 over the Continental Divide into the Rio Grande Drainage area. At about 6 miles from the top the Bear Town/Kite Lake Road departs to the right. Follow this road across the stream for 7 miles to Kite Lake. The road ends on the far side of the lake, so you will need to backtrack to the Stony Pass Road to continue your journey.

Index

Notes

Notes

Notes

Notes